6|10

Please check all items for damages
before leaving the Library.
Thereafter you will be held
responsible for all injuries
to items beyond reasonable wear.

APR   200

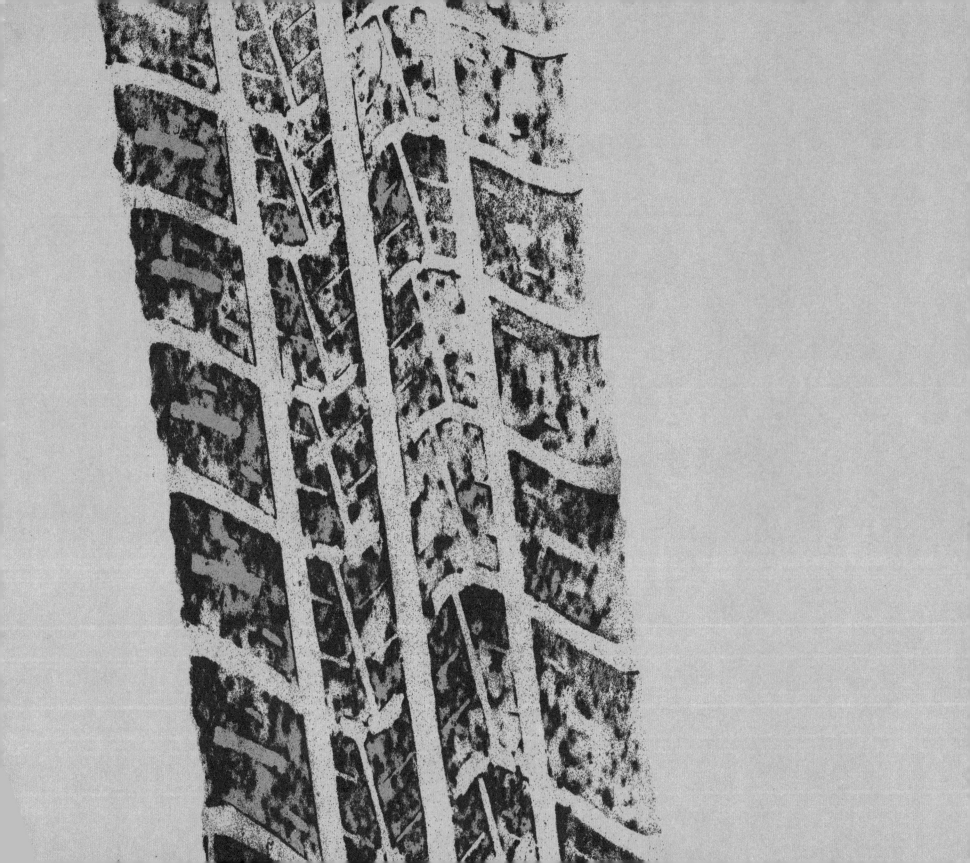

I DRIVE A DUMP TRUCK

by **Sarah Bridges**

illustrated by **Derrick Alderman** & **Denise Shea**

PICTURE WINDOW BOOKS
Minneapolis, Minnesota

Thanks to Local Union 49 in Rosemount, Minnesota (especially Gene Sebion)—S.B.

Thanks to our advisers for their expertise, research, and advice:

Tom Jackson, Executive Editor of *Equipment World*
Tuscaloosa, Alabama

Susan Kesselring, M.A., Literacy Educator
Rosemount-Apple Valley-Eagan (Minnesota) School District

Managing Editors: Bob Temple, Catherine Neitge
Creative Director: Terri Foley
Editors: Brenda Haugen, Christianne Jones
Editorial Adviser: Andrea Cascardi
Designer: Nathan Gassman
Storyboard development: Amy Bailey Muehlenhardt
Page production: Banta Digital Group
The illustrations in this book were rendered digitally.

Picture Window Books
5115 Excelsior Boulevard, Suite 232
Minneapolis, MN 55416
877-845-8392
www.picturewindowbooks.com

Printed in the United States of America.

Library of Congress Cataloging-in-Publication Data
Bridges, Sarah.
I drive a dump truck / by Sarah Bridges ; illustrated by
    Derrick Alderman and Denise Shea.
p. cm. — (Working wheels)
Includes bibliographical references and index.
ISBN 1-4048-0614-8 (reinforced library binding : alk. paper)
1. Dump trucks—Juvenile literature. [1. Dump trucks.
    2. Trucks. 3. Earthmoving machinery.] I. Alderman,
    Derrick, ill. II. Shea, Denise, ill. III. Title. IV. Series.
TL230.15.B74 2004
629.225—dc22
                                                    2003028225

3

My name is Henry, and I drive a dump truck. I check my truck carefully before starting work for the day.

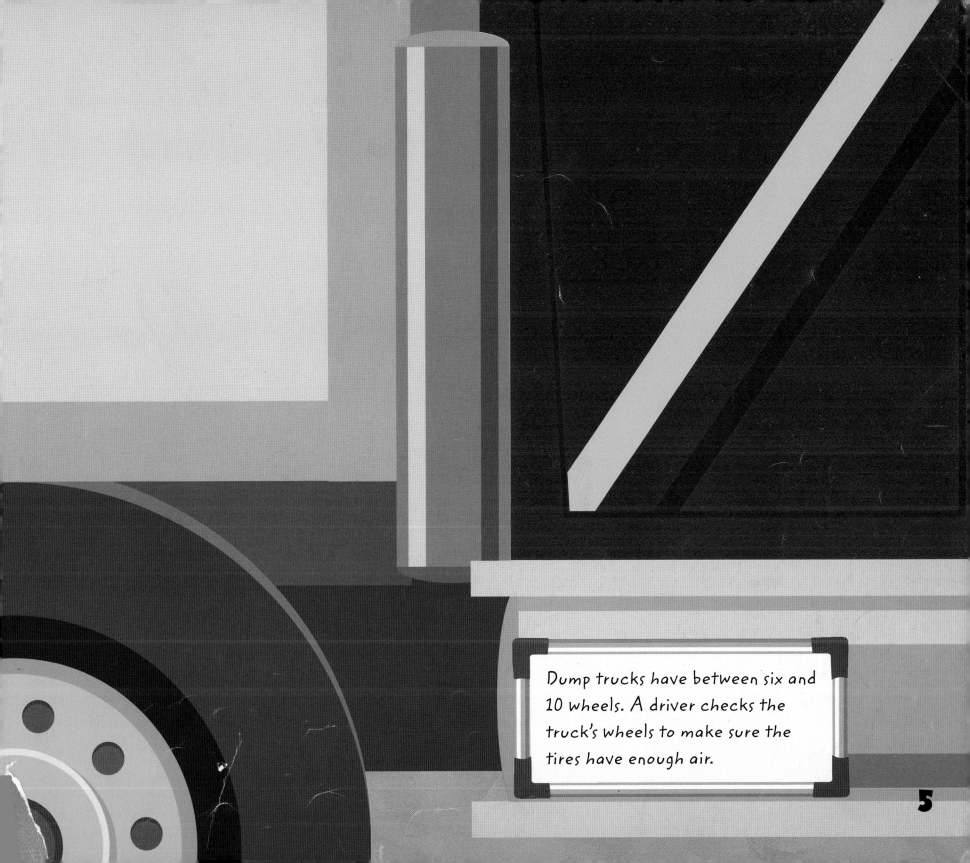

Dump trucks have between six and 10 wheels. A driver checks the truck's wheels to make sure the tires have enough air.

My truck has a special air system that
makes the brakes work.

The air system makes a loud **Choosh** sound when the brakes are ready.

A buzzer rings if the air system is not ready. It sounds like a loud doorbell.

My truck has three mirrors. Two are attached outside the passenger's seat. One is found outside the driver's seat.

The mirrors help me back up without **hitting** anything.

The small, round mirror on the passenger side is called the peep sight. It lets the driver peep around the truck.

My truck's main job is to haul things from one place to another.

A wheel loader empties dirt, rocks, or fill into my dump box.

10

The biggest dump truck can carry about 45,000 pounds (20,412 kilograms). That's more than the weight of four elephants!

Sometimes, my truck is loaded
with gravel from quarries. Gravel
is used for making roads.

Dump trucks have hoist levers that make
the dump box go up. As the dump box
rises, the tailgate opens. Then everything
spills out of the dump box.

When my truck is full, I drive the gravel to another spot and dump it out.

Sometimes dirt is too **mushy** to build things on.

Wheel loaders scoop up the soft dirt. They load the dirt into the dump box. I haul the soil away.

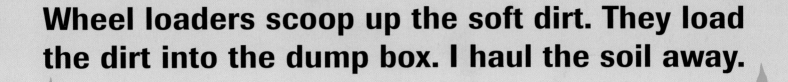

Dirt may be bad for one thing but good for another. Mushy, squishy dirt can be hard to build on, but it is great for gardens and backyards.

My truck has a special cab shield
that protects me.

Sometimes, heavy things are mixed into the dirt that is poured into my truck.

The cab shield prevents heavy things from landing on the driver. It is like a big metal hood over the truck's cab.

Sometimes my truck hauls 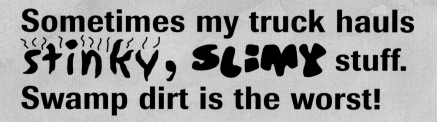 stuff. Swamp dirt is the worst!

Stinky, slimy jobs are called mucker jobs. Not many drivers like to do mucker jobs.

After a messy job, the driver needs to clean out the truck with a shovel. Otherwise the muck will mix with the dirt and rock from the next job.

19

After my truck is emptied, I lower the dump box again. If I forget to do this, my dump box could hit an overpass!

I'm done for the day. It's time to put my dump truck away.

After the last load, the driver lowers the box, locks the tail latch, and turns off the system that lets the dump box go up and down.

DUMP TRUCK DIAGRAM

cab shield

cab

tailgate

dump box

GLOSSARY

cab—the place where the driver of the dump truck sits

cab shield—the unit that protects the cab and the driver

dump box—the part of the dump truck that holds the dirt and other materials

fill—a mix of rock, sand, dirt, or clay

quarry—a place where stone or gravel is dug out of the ground

tailgate—a gate on the back of a dump truck that can be opened when the driver wants to empty the dump box

tail latch—the lever that opens and locks the tailgate

FUN FACTS

 Dump trucks have bells or buzzers on their back bumpers or frames that ring when they back up. This tells people to get out of the way.

 Dump trucks used to be smaller than they are today. They often pulled a second trailer, or box, behind them. The two vehicles were called a truck and a pup.

 After a lot of use, roads sink down and need to be built back up. Dump trucks haul in gravel and hot asphalt to help build the roads up again.

 Drivers can't see out the back window of a dump truck because of the cab shield. A light inside the dump truck tells the driver if the dump box is up.

 Sometimes a snowplow is hooked to the front of a dump truck. After the snow is pushed into a pile, a wheel loader scoops the snow into the box of the dump truck to be hauled away.

TO LEARN MORE

At the Library

Dahl, Michael. *One Big Building: A Counting Book About Construction.* Minneapolis: Picture Window Books, 2004.

Jango-Cohen, Judith. *Dump Trucks.* Minneapolis: Lerner, 2003.

Randolph, Joanne. *Dump Trucks.* New York: Powerkids Press, 2002.

Teitelbaum, Michael. *If I Could Drive a Dump Truck!* New York: Scholastic, 2001.

On the Web

FactHound offers a safe, fun way to find Web sites related to this book. All of the sites on FactHound have been researched by our staff. www.facthound.com

1. Visit the FactHound home page.

2. Enter a search word related to this book, or type in this special code: 1404806148.

3. Click on the FETCH IT button.

Your trusty FactHound will fetch the best Web sites for you!

INDEX

BOOKS IN THIS SERIES

- I Drive an Ambulance
- I Drive a Bulldozer
- I Drive a Dump Truck
- I Drive a Garbage Truck
- I Drive a Semitruck
- I Drive a Snowplow

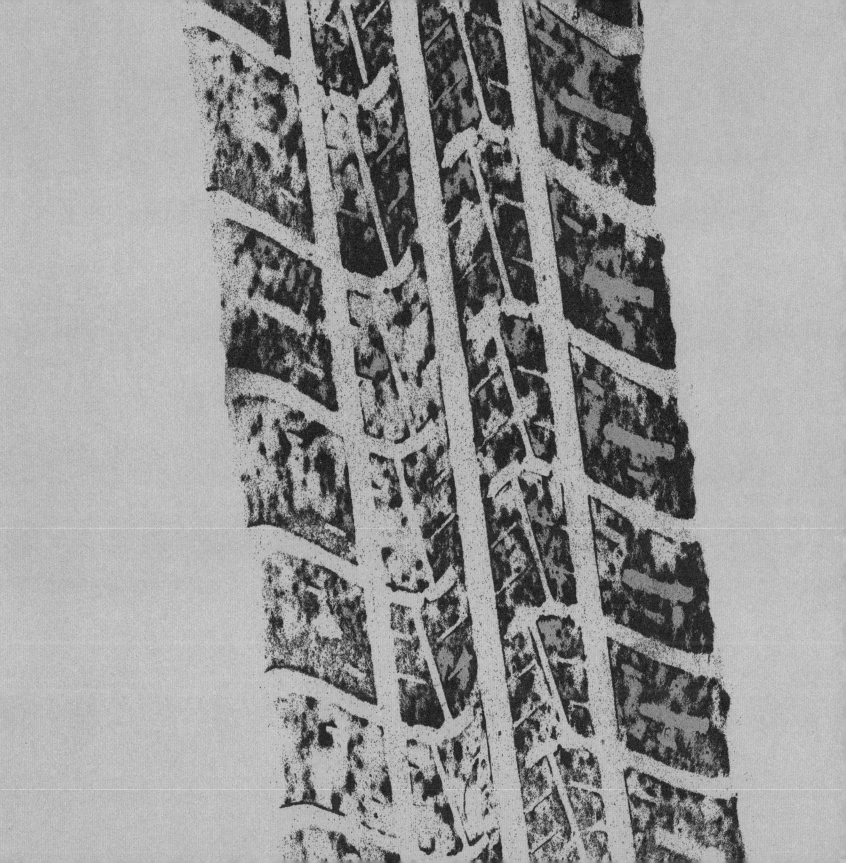